FISHING

Ang

L

Illustrated by Fran Lee

GIBBS·SMITH
P
PUBLISHER

Salt Lake City

First Edition
02 01 00 99   5 4 3 2 1
Text copyright © 1999 G. Lawson Drinkard III
Illustrations and Design copyright © 1999 Fran Lee

Disclaimer: The publisher and author warn that there is inherent danger in
the sport of fishing and that children should <u>always</u> be supervised by a
responsible adult when fishing. The publisher and author bear no
responsibility or liability for injuries or property damage that may result
from fishing or participating in any activities described in this book.

Published by
Gibbs Smith, Publisher
P.O. Box 667
Layton, Utah 84041
Orders (800) 748-5439
www.gibbs-smith.com

Printed in Hong Kong

Library of Congress Cataloging-in-Publication Data

Drinkard, G. Lawson, 1951-
    Fishing in a brook / G. Lawson Drinkard, III ; illustrations by Fran Lee
        p. cm.
    ISBN 0-87905-940-0
    1. Fishing Juvenile literature.   I. Title.
SH445.D75 2000
799.1—dc21

99-36731
CIP

To my father, Lawson,
who taught me to fish,
and to Harry and Bob,
who got me started again.
—GLD

To my brother, David Lee,
and his family,
Laurie and Stefanie.
Catch and Release.
—FL

CONTENTS

Other Activities and Adventures

INTRODUCTION

I DON'T REMEMBER at what age I started to fish. I only know that I've been fishing as long as I can remember. I'm quite sure the first person to take me fishing was my dad, who was a kind, patient, and knowledge-able teacher. Sometimes we fished in streams and sometimes in lakes, sometimes from boats and sometimes from the bank, sometimes for trout and sometimes for bluegill. Usually we took day trips but occasionally we'd go camping—and fish-ing! My childhood memories are filled with fishing-related activities, like the opening day of trout season, with fish caught and the ones that got away, fishing lures made during the winter, a fishing rod for Christmas, and time spent sitting in a canoe and talking with my dad, just waiting for the fish to bite.

Fishing is an activity that can be enjoyed by just about anyone—young and old, male and female, short and tall, and by those who are physically blessed and those who have some physical challenges. No matter who you are or how you are, there is a place in fishing for you.

Fishing is a hopeful sport. "I hope the weather is good tomorrow." "I think I'll catch some fish today." "I know I'll enjoy your company while we fish together."

Fishing is a thoughtful sport. "I wonder what kind of bug that is." "I think the fish will be biting at 8:00 tomorrow morning." "I believe we should clean up this trash and protect this stream habitat."

Fishing is about patience. Sometimes the fish aren't biting and you just have to wait until they are.

Fishing is about science. You have to know something about wildlife, insects, fish, and water to be successful.

Fishing is about responsibility. You learn to obey fishing regulations, practice water safety, and protect our environment.

Always, always, fishing should be about fun. There is pure joy in waking up in the morning, heading out to your favorite fishing spot, and taking time to notice, enjoy, and be thankful for all nature has to offer.

This book offers you an introduction to a lifelong journey of discovery. If you have never fished before, there are new skills to master and much to learn. Even after you have fished for more than forty years, you will learn something new each time you fish—if you are attentive.

So, read and learn, develop good fishing habits, be careful, have fun always and . . . go fishing!

LET'S GO FISHING!

What is Fishing?

THIS BOOK IS ABOUT SPORT FISHING, or catching fish for fun. It's always important to remember when you are fishing for fun, don't make it into work!

Why Go Fishing?

Here is a list of possible reasons:

- **To be outdoors.** Fishing takes you away from the TV, telephone, video games, refrigerator, and other indoor distractions. It's a way to just enjoy being outside and appreciate all that Mother Nature has to offer.

- **To spend time alone.** Sometimes you just need to get away, be by yourself and think. Fish don't talk much, and if the catching is slow, it gives you time to think about other things.

- **To spend time with someone else.** A fishing trip is a great reason to take family or buddies and spend some time outdoors together. Planning is half the fun. Figuring out where to go, what to bring, what to wear, etc., can give you hours of pleasure—and that doesn't even include the fishing!

To observe and learn about nature. Fish are wild creatures. The more you learn about them and their habitat, the more successful you will be when you go fishing. For instance, lots of fish eat insects, so, many accomplished fishermen pursue the study of entomology (the scientific study of insects).

To see different parts of the world. Fish are found everywhere, and although you can go across the fence or to the next county, eventually you'll want to go to some faraway stream in another state or another country. Fishing is a great excuse to plan a trip to Belize, Brazil, Bimini, or the Bahamas!

To exercise your brain. Though fish have very small brains compared to those of humans, their survival instincts drive them to be pretty smart when it comes to not getting caught. In order to outsmart the fish, one has to learn the ways of a particular fish: where it lives, what it eats, when it eats, how it hides, and what it uses for cover. Learning theset hings about particular kinds of fish takes time and energy but pays off when you outsmart a fish.

To catch fish. There is nothing quite as exciting as feeling the tug of a hooked fish on your line. There is mystery involved—you don't know what kind or how big it is until you've cranked it to the surface. There is skill involved—it takes some skill to land a fish, especially a big one. Sometimes there is disappointment—you may lose the big one before you get it in the net.

Can you think of some more reasons to go fishing?

Fun Fish Facts

Fish are among the oldest living creatures on the earth (under the water!). Scientists tell us that the first primitive ones appeared around 510 million years ago, and "modern" fish with bones and vertebrae as we know them now evolved around 395 million years ago. By comparison, people have inhabited the earth for only around 4 million years.

Fish come in all sizes, shapes, and colors. Some adult fish are only $\frac{1}{2}$ inch long and weigh less than $\frac{1}{10}$ of an ounce. A few are as big as 60 feet long and weigh more than 20 tons. Fish come in a rainbow of colors. Some fish are green, some are brown, some are black, and some are orange.

There are more than 20,000 kinds of fish living in the world's oceans, lakes, streams, rivers, and ponds.

Fish live at altitudes of more than three miles above sea level (in high mountain lakes) and at depths more than six miles below sea level (in the oceans). They live in waters with temperatures higher than 100 degrees F., and lower than 32 degrees F. They thrive virtually everywhere on the earth except for waters that have become too polluted to support aquatic life and waters that are too salty, such as the Dead Sea and the Great Salt Lake.

WHERE CAN I FISH?

Water, Water Everywhere

WITHOUT FAIL, you will find that fish live in the water. Unlike mammals, they don't have lungs to take in oxygen, so they don't breathe like people do. Instead, their bodies get oxygen by taking it from the water that flows through their gills. They can survive for a few minutes outside the water but not for very long. So, to know something about where to fish, you have to know something about water—the place fish live.

Finding A Freshwater Place to Fish

You may be lucky enough to live within walking distance of a fishable pond, lake, or stream. If not, you'll want to find an adult fishing pal who can drive the two of you to a fishing spot.

You will find lakes, ponds and streams on private land and in municipal (that means city-owned), state, and national parks. If asked nicely, many private landowners will give you permission to fish on their property, and most public waters are open to fishing with certain restrictions and regulations. To find places to fish in your area, the people in a bait and tackle shop or a good sports store can be a great source of information. Most states have a Department of Game and Inland Fisheries (or some similarly named office) that regulates fishing and will be able to give you detailed information on places to fish, fishing licenses, seasons, and rules.

If you have a chapter of Trout Unlimited in your area, try to get in touch with one of its members, who will certainly know where to fish for trout and may be able to tell you about special regulation areas set aside just for kids. Maybe the group sponsors a "Take A Kid Fishing Day."

Fishing in Salt Water

If you live near one of the coasts or if your family takes a vacation to the beach, you might have an opportunity to fish in salt water. Thousands of kinds of fish live in the ocean. Some are quite small, and some are very, very large. One of the exciting things about saltwater fishing is that you never know just what kind of creature you might catch or how big it might be!

As you can imagine, with so many different kinds and sizes of fish the ocean has to offer, there are also dozens of different ways to fish for them. Here are several you might be able to try on your own or with an adult fishing buddy.

Surf Fishing

The place where the waves tumble or crash onto the beach at the ocean or bay is known as the surf. Depending upon where you are, the water in the surf can be very shallow, or the sand under the water can drop off and the

water can be very deep. Also, because of the tides, the depth of the water will always be rising or falling, depending on the time of day and the time of month. That's one of the fun and interesting things about tides—the times for high and low tides change every day.

To catch fish in the surf you will need a rod and reel that allow you to cast your baited line with a fairly heavy sinker out into the waves. These surf-casting rods are usually six to ten feet long and are heavy enough to allow a one- or two-ounce sinker to be tossed quite a ways out into the water. If you can't borrow such a rig from a friend, there are usually bait and tackle shops near the shore that rent tackle on a daily basis. They are also good places to ask advice about where to fish, what to fish for, when to fish, and what kind of bait to use for a particular fish. Of course, they sell bait too!

Some of the kinds of fish you might catch in the surf include sea bass, croakers, spot, ocean perch, sea trout, bluefish, flounder, or even a small shark. Bait can include cut fish, cut squid, minnows, and artificial lures.

When you go surf fishing, be sure not to venture too far out into the waves while trying to get your bait farther from the shore, and if you are fishing at a beach where others are swimming, be careful not to accidentally "catch" a person.

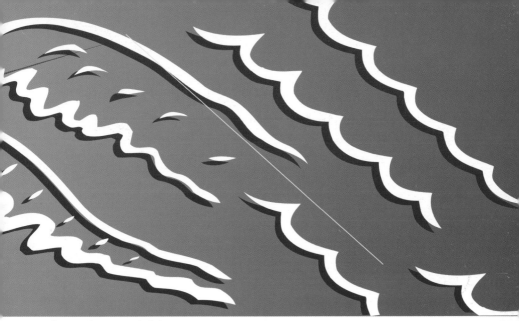

Dock and Pier Fishing

Many coastal areas have long piers extending far out into the water beyond the beach and crashing waves of the surf. These piers are built especially for fishing, and there is usually a modest charge for using the facility. Many have bait and tackle shops where you can rent equipment, buy bait, and seek free advice about the fishing.

In every coastal area along the edges of the bays, harbors, and sounds, you will find docks where people tie their commercial and pleasure-fishing boats. Though there are not usually big fish around these docks, it can be lots of fun to fish for the little ones that are almost always around. This is a place where you can use just a piece of fishing line with a hook and sinker on the end, or you can use your homemade fishing pole. Almost anything will work for bait: pieces of cheese, bologna, hot dog, raw bacon, corn, squashed-together bread, or any other natural fishing baits like worms, minnows, etc. Just plunk your line over the edge of the dock and wait for the action to begin.

PLEASE!

If it is a private dock you want to use, ask permission before you begin to fish, and don't climb aboard anyone's boat unless you are invited.

Charter-Boat Fishing

In almost all coastal areas, there are people who make their living by taking other people out fishing on their boats. These boats are called charter boats. A charter fishing trip can be very exciting, and depending upon where you go, you may have the opportunity to catch some really big fish like marlin, tuna, dolphin, and sharks! Sometimes these trips can be quite expensive, but there is one particular kind of charter boat that is less costly. It is usually called a "party boat" because it is rather large and holds lots of people who want to fish. Because there are so many people on board, and because they don't go so far out into the ocean, the cost per person is less.

WHAT DO I NEED?

NOW THAT YOU KNOW a little something about water, fish, and places to go fishing, it's probably time to get to the main topic—going fishing!

Though fishing can become complicated with fancy lures, expensive reels, shiny boats, water-depth finders, and all sorts of other gadgets, all you really need to fish is a pole, some line, a sinker, a bobber, a hook, and some bait. So, let's organize what we need for a simple and successful fishing trip to your local pond. The next few pages explain what you need for rigging your pole.

Basic Rigging Equipment

Fishing Pole

A fishing pole (also called a fishing rod) can be made from a small tree or branch. The best kind of wood is fairly stiff but with some "bend" to it. Your pole should be five to six feet long and taper gently (grow thinner) along its length. Bamboo makes excellent fishing poles, but most any wood will do. Cut a slight notch at the end of the pole for a place to tie and anchor your fishing line.

You can also purchase a fishing rod at a sporting goods, bait and tackle, or chain discount store. They will probably have some inexpensive ones made of bamboo or fiberglass.

Fishing Line

Most fishing line is made of nylon and is called "monofilament," or mono for short. It comes on spools of various lengths that are called "tests." Usually, a four-pound test line will hold up a fish weighing four pounds without breaking. The larger the test of the line, the thicker the diameter it is and the more it will hold. For your basic rig, try to find a piece of four-pound or six-pound test line that is eight to ten feet long. Tie the line onto the end of your pole. Now you're making progress!

Sinkers

A sinker is a weight tied to the end of your line that makes the line and bait sink into the water where the fish are. Store-bought sinkers are usually made of lead and come in many different shapes, sizes, and weights. The depth of the water and the speed of the current will determine how much weight you need to hold your bait in front of a hungry fish.

One easy sinker to use is called a split shot. It is a small round piece of lead with a slit in it. To attach the sinker, just slide your line through the slit and squeeze the lead together.

Egg sinker

Split shot

Use your fingers or a pair of pliers, but DON'T use your teeth! Besides the possibility of damaging your teeth, lead is poisonous and shouldn't be put into your mouth.) To add more weight to your line, just add more split shot.

Another kind of weight is called an egg sinker. It is made of lead, shaped like a chicken egg, and has a hole through the middle. To use an egg sinker, run your line through the hole and place a split shot below the sinker to hold it in place. An egg sinker will attach more weight to the line, but when the fish takes your bait it won't feel the weight because the line slips through the sinker.

Bobbers

A sinker takes your bait to the desired depth in the water, and a bobber holds it at that level. Bobbers come in various sizes to accommodate different sinkers and baits. They are usually made of red and white plastic and have a push-button spring attachment that makes moving them up and down your line easy.

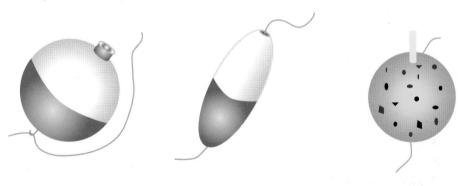

You can make your own bobber using a bottle cork. Make a *slit* along the side of the cork halfway through the cork. Then, just slide it on your line; the friction of the cork on the line should hold it in place.

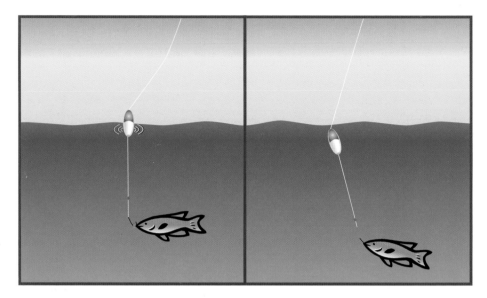

The bobber has a second benefit. When the bobber twitches in the water, you know a fish is nibbling at your bait. When it goes under the water, you know a fish is serious about eating the bait and it's time to "set the hook" (give the line a little jerk).

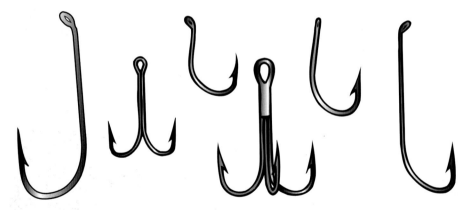

Hooks

Fishing hooks come in all shapes and sizes. They are probably the most important part of your fishing equipment, but luckily they are not very expensive. It's a good idea to have a small assortment of hooks for various fishing situations.

A basic fishing hook is shaped like the letter "J" and is made up of several parts. They are called the eye, the shank, the bend, the barb, and the point. The eye is where you tie the hook onto your line. The point is what you use to put on the bait, and what penetrates the mouth of the fish when it eats the bait. The barb is shaped such that after the hook goes into the fish's mouth, it won't easily come back out. Many people who are fishing just for fun (not for the frying pan) make what is known as a barbless hook. With a pair of pliers, they mash down the barb. Though you don't always land as many fish, these hooks are a lot more "fish friendly," and they make it much easier to release what you catch.

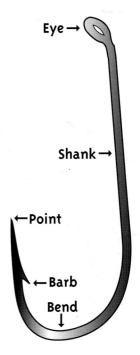

Generally, large hooks are for large fish and small hooks are for small fish. You should choose a hook appropriate for the weight of fish you will be trying to catch. You might begin with a size 4 or 6, but if you are going for the big fish, you might need something larger. An experienced fisherman friend can give you some help with this.

The point of your hook should be sharp, for good reason: so you can hook the fish! If it gets dull or a little rusty, it won't catch as many fish. Get a file and re-sharpen it.

When handling hooks, be careful not to hook yourself. Press the points into an old cork or soft piece of wood so they won't prick you. Store the hooks in your tackle box.

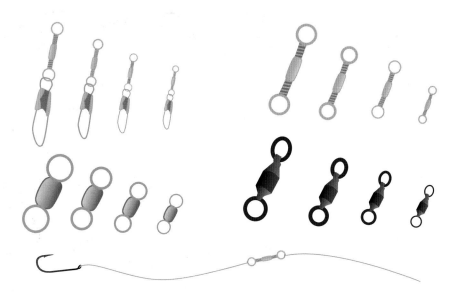

Swivels

Another piece of tackle called a swivel comes in handy if you are using bait (like a minnow) or a lure (like a spinner) that has a twisting or turning action that tends to get your line twisted. Tie a swivel between your bait and your line. This will allow the bait or lure to spin without getting the line all tangled up. Swivels are inexpensive and come in various sizes to match the hooks and lures you might be using.

Rigging Your Pole

All that's left now is to put your pieces of tackle together, put on your bait, and go fishing! After you've tied your line onto the end of your pole, there are several ways to rig the other end. One way is to tie the hook onto the end of the line, come up several inches and squeeze on your sinker, and put your bobber on above that.

Another method, called a fish-finder rig, puts the weight at the bottom of the line with the hook tied off to the side on an extra piece of line. This kind of rig lets the bait float freely and naturally in the water (a better way to fool the fish) while the sinker holds it at the correct depth.

Once your pole is rigged, you'll need to decide what kind of "food" to put on your hook to attract the fish.

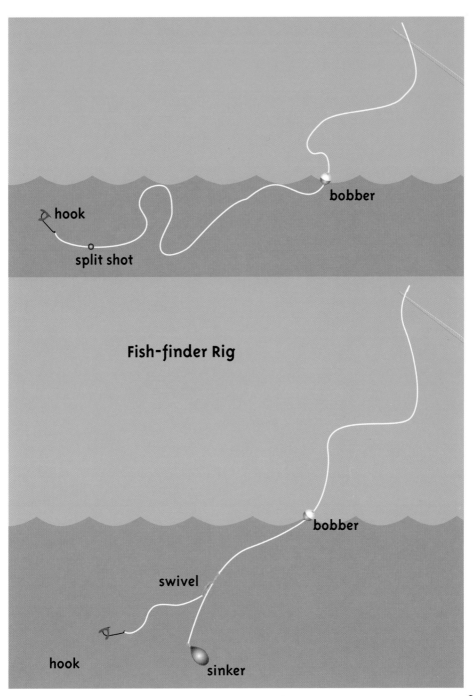

hook

split shot

bobber

Fish-finder Rig

bobber

swivel

hook

sinker

23

Baits and Lures

Bait is what you put on the end of your line to attract the fish, something a fish would love to eat. Just like people, all fish are not attracted to the same foods. Some baits work better than others for certain types of fish. (See the fish food charts on pages 50–56.)

Bait can be broken down into two major types: 1) live or natural bait, and 2) artificial bait and lures.

Live and Natural Bait

There are a number of living creatures that many fish like to eat. These include earthworms, minnows (tiny fish), crickets, grasshoppers, and crayfish. All of these baits can be gathered for free. Worms can be dug in your garden, grasshoppers collected in grassy fields, crickets found in dark corners in the basement (beware of spiders!), crayfish found under rocks in small creeks, and minnows seined or caught in a minnow trap at a local pond.

A Slimy Worm Safari

The lowly earthworm is the most reliable bait in places where angling is allowed. And fat, juicy worms are pretty easy to find. Here's how it's done:

1. Grab a shovel—any size will do. Take along a bucket or can big enough to hold a few worms with dirt.

2. For a daytime hunt, dig around in cool, moist spots like these: a compost heap, vegetable or flower garden, a pile of old manure.

3. For a night crawler safari, bring along a flashlight. These fat, juicy worms can be found near the surface of the ground, especially after a gentle rain. Look on the lawn, in a park, along ditch banks, in fields.

4. Store your worms in moist (but not soggy) dirt and keep them cool. The refrigerator is okay for a few days. Just be sure to label the container so Mom won't grab them for breakfast!

Building a Seine

Building a small seine (net) to catch minnows (very small fish) is quite an easy project. Find two sticks 3 feet long and an inch or so in diameter. Also, find a piece of cheesecloth or old plastic window screen about 2 feet by 3 feet. Wrap and tack the ends of the narrower sides of the net material securely to each of the sticks. You are done!

At a shallow place in a pond or creek, scoop up some minnows for bait. Keep them in a bucket full of fresh cool water so they will stay healthy.

Entomology

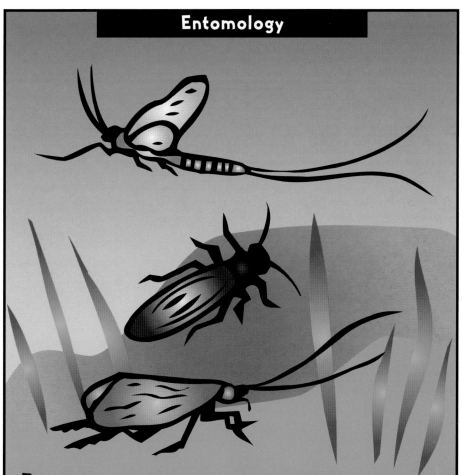

Entomology is the study of insects. The diets of a good many fish include insects.

To be a successful angler, you won't have to learn all 750,000 insect species. Just a dozen or so that fish like to eat will do nicely. Especially when fishing for trout, a working knowledge of mayflies, caddisflies, and stoneflies will greatly improve your enjoyment in observing and catching fish. One very good book to check out is called **STREAMSIDE GUIDE TO NATURALS AND THEIR ARTIFICIALS,** by Art Flick. It is filled with photographs of real flies and the artificial flies that you can use to imitate the natural ones.

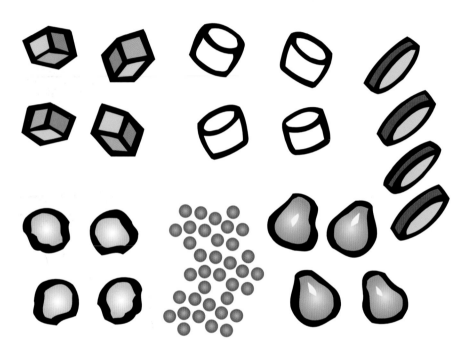

Other natural baits include corn kernels, pieces of hot dog, marshmallows, salmon eggs, cheese, and dough balls. Most of these can be found in your pantry or made from ingredients you have there. Salmon eggs can be purchased at a bait and tackle store. Not too many marshmallows grow in nature, but for some reason certain types of fish like them!

All of these natural baits can be used with your homemade fishing pole. Choose your bait based on the type of fish you are trying to catch (see fish-bait chart on pages 50–56). Put the bait on your hook, toss it into the water, and wait for the fish to bite. If you just can't decide which bait to use, a worm is always a good bet for most types of fish.

Artificial Bait and Lures

In fishing lingo, artificial bait is usually called a lure. Some lures closely imitate living creatures such as worms, flies, frogs, and minnows. Other lures attract fish by their movement and their sound or by tempting the fish's curiosity. There are hundreds of different types of artificial lures, but many come under the basic categories of plugs, poppers, spoons, jigs, or spinners.

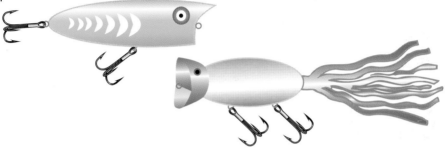

Plugs are designed to look something like a small fish. Some are made to float and some are made to dive down into the water. They shimmy, shake, gurgle, and splash in various ways to imitate something a hungry fish would like to eat.

Poppers imitate bugs floating on the surface of the water. When twitched along, they make a sort of "glub" sound that attracts certain kinds of fish.

The Rules about Bait

Most places allow you to fish with live and natural baits, but certain special-regulation areas require that you use only artificial lures. Some areas even require that your hooks be barbless. If you are in one of those areas, be sure to follow the rules.

Spoons look something like the eating end of a teaspoon. They are heavier than water, and imitate a speedy minnow flashing and darting under the surface as they are reeled in.

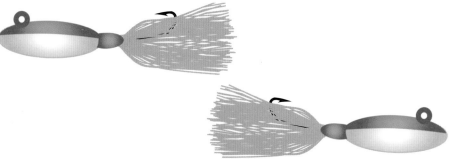

Jigs are small hooks weighted with lead near the eye of the hook. They are often decorated with feathers, artificial eyes, rubber legs, and tinsel. They are cast into the water and "jigged," or bounced up and down, to attract the fish.

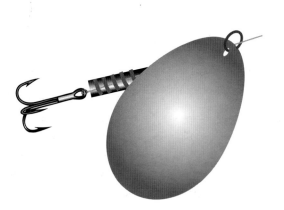

Spinners have small blades or propellers that rotate around a center shaft. When you drag a spinner through the water, the blade spins and flashes, attracting fish by the motion it makes and the vibrations it sends into the water.

Rods and Reels

In order to be most effective, almost all of the artificial lures should be used on certain kinds of store-bought fishing rods with reels attached. There are bait-casting rods for bait and plugs, fly rods for artificial flies and poppers, and spinning rods for spoons, jigs, and spinners. Different types of reels are made for each of these rods, but all of them hold a spool of line and allow the lure to be cast out into the water and reeled back in.

Tackle Box

Your tackle box is a place to collect and store all of your different kinds of fishing equipment. It holds the gear you'll need to catch various kinds of fish, and it represents a world of fishing dreams and possibilities.

Most any durable box with a tight lid and a handle will work for holding your tackle. An old toolbox, sewing box, or an artist's paint box can be easily adapted. In a pinch, even a shoe box will do. Most sporting goods stores sell tackle boxes in a variety of sizes and price ranges. When considering the size of your tackle box, remember that fishing is a lifelong pursuit. You'll always be adding to your tackle collection, and it's unlikely that you'll ever throw away a lure. In other words, buy a box bigger than you think you'll need, because eventually you'll fill it.

Tackle Box Checklist

- A variety of hooks
- Bobbers in various sizes
- Lures *(you'll collect lots over time)*
- Fish knife
- Fish scaler *(if you plan to clean and cook your fish)*
- Extra fishing line
- A spare reel
- File *(for sharpening the points on your hooks)*
- Weights in different shapes & sizes
- Hook disgorger *(for removing hook from your fish)*
- Needle-nose pliers
- Swivels
- Fish stringer *(if you plan to keep your fish)*
- A couple of small adhesive bandages *(guess who these are for?!)*
- Sunscreen
- Fish scales *(for weighing your fish)*
- A pen or pencil *(for making notes)*

After using your tackle box for a while you'll discover how to arrange your gear so it's easy to find. If you have a collection of plastic worms, don't mix these with your other tackle or place them directly in the plastic trays of your box. For some reason, they seem to cause other plastics to melt and stick together. Get a "worm box" from your tackle shop or store them in a plastic sandwich bag that zips closed. Be creative about storage possibilities. Discarded film canisters make excellent places to keep small weights or lures. Pill bottles or plastic food containers also come in handy

It's not usually a good idea to store your bait in your tackle box. If you leave that can of worms or crickets in there for a month or two, your tackle box will smell worse than a dead fish next time you open it!

Knots to Know

There are many different skills associated with being successful at fishing. One of them is the art of tying good knots. Monofilament fishing line stretches and is kind of slippery, so using the proper knot is important if you want to keep your bait, lure, or fish on the line.

Knots are fun to learn, and using the right one for the right purpose will let others know that you are skilled at the art of fishing.

Here are a couple of knots worth learning:

Clinch Knot (or Fisherman's Knot)

This knot is used for that most important place—where the hook (or the swivel or the lure) meets the line. A reliable knot here will save you lots of lost lures and fish.

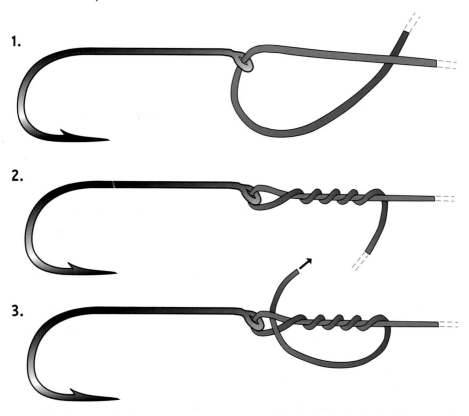

1.

2.

3.

4.

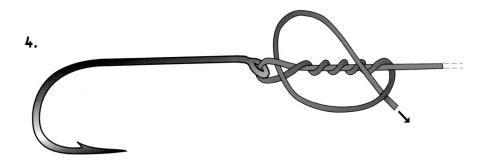

5.

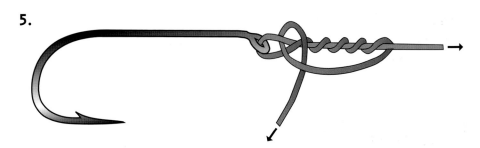

6.

1. Run several inches of line through the hook eye. Don't be stingy here. Make it comfortable and easy to tie.
2. Wrap the loose end of your line around itself five or six times.
3. Pass the loose end through the loop in the line next to the eye in the hook.
4. Push the loose end through the new loop you just created. Wet the knot with a little spit. This will lubricate the line and make your knot easier to tighten.
5. Tighten the knot slowly by pulling on the line with one hand and the hook with the other.
6. Trim off the loose end of the line with a pair of fingernail clippers.

Surgeon's Knot

A surgeon's knot is used to tie two pieces of fishing line together—usually a shorter piece to a longer piece. For example, you might use this knot to tie some extra line (called tippet) onto the end of your fly-line leader.

1.

2.

3.

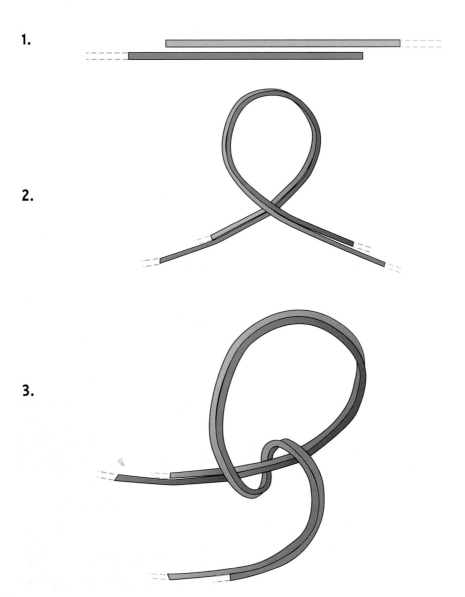

4.

5.

1. Hold the two pieces of line so they line up; keep a 6- to 8-inch overlap.
2. Holding your fingers near the ends of the overlap, make a loop in the line.
3. While pinching this loop together with one hand, wrap the two loose ends of the line around the loop twice, like an overhand knot tied twice.
4. Spit on the loop, then gently tighten it by pulling evenly from both ends of the line.
5. Trim off the loose end of the line with a pair of fingernail clippers.

Other fishing knots include a perfection loop, a dropper loop, a turle knot, a figure-eight knot, a blood knot, and an anchor knot.

If you are interested in learning more about knots, ask a good fisherman to teach you, or pick up a book at the library.

Fishing Expedition Checklist

- **Lunch** *(keep your food and worms fresh in a cooler)*
- **Drinking water**
- **Bait** *(bring extra toavoid the frustration of running out if the fish are biting)*
- **Fishing pole or hand line** *(pretty obvious if you're going fishing!)*
- **Life jacket** *(if you will be in a boat, on a steep bank, or standing in swift water)*
- **Fishing hat** *(to keep the sun off of your head and face—and sometimes a handy place to keep your fishing lures)*
- **Sunglasses** *(polarized glasses make it easier to see the fish under the water)*
- **Insect repellent**
- **Knife and pliers** *(to cut fish line, bait, remove hooks, and cut your cheese for lunch)*
- **Tackle box** *(to carry all of your favorite lures, bobbers, weights, and hooks)*
- **Permission to fish** *(Always, ALWAYS ask first)*
- **Fishing log or journal** *(to record the date, time, weather, size, and number of fish you catch—perhaps even to draw a sketch of the big one)*
- **Camera** *(to capture photos of you, your fish, and your friend's fish)*

HOW DO I FISH?

Baiting Your Hook

IN ORDER TO CATCH FISH, you'll need to have some bait on your hook. You can put it on just any old way, but like lots of things in life, you'll have more success if you learn to do it right.

Live bait (worms, minnows, crickets, grasshoppers, etc.) should always appear to the fish to be alive. When you put them on your hook, they will die eventually, but you want them to look like they are alive. This will make them a more appealing meal to the fish.

Some people don't like to kill things like worms and minnows in order to catch fish. If you are one of those persons, that's okay. Just use baits like cheese, corn, dough balls, or salmon eggs. Of course, you can also learn to use artificial lures to solve this dilemma.

Following are a couple of diagrams showing ways to bait your hook with worms, minnows, and insects.

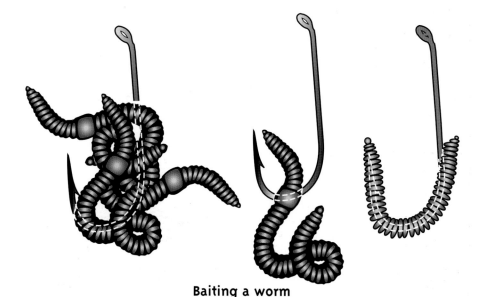

Baiting a worm

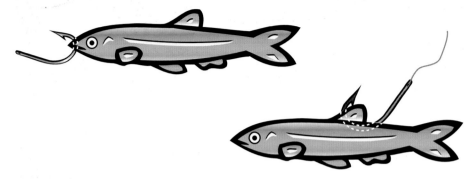

Baiting a minnow

Baiting a cricket or grasshopper

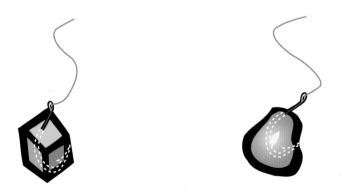

Baiting corn or cheese

Casting Your Bait

Putting your bait in front of a hungry fish will often allow you to feel that exciting tug of a bite at the end of your line. Sometimes an accurate cast will make all of the difference in whether you catch fish or not. Learning how to get your bait or lure to the right place may take some practice, but it will be worth it.

Casting your fishing pole is about the easiest thing you'll do all day. Since you will only have a few feet of line attached, you can just hold your pole out over the bank of the pond (or the edge of the dock or the side of the boat) and drop your baited hook in. If you have a little more line attached, you can swing your pole gently toward the water in a motion like batting a baseball. The line and weight will follow out into the water. Be careful not to hook yourself or someone else.

Overhead cast

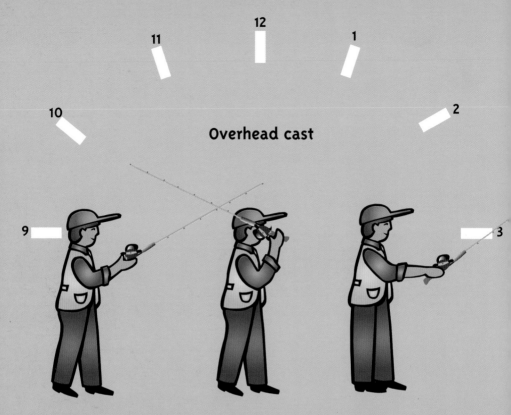

There are two standard ways to cast a bait-casting or spinning rod—the overhead cast and the side-arm cast. Both use the same motion, but one is done vertically (overhead), and one is done horizontally (out to the side). You should practice and become proficient at both. Fishing conditions will determine which method to use. If there are overhanging trees where you are fishing, the side-arm cast would save you some frustration. If you are standing on a dock or boat between two other people, the overhead cast would be a smart choice.

For the overhead cast use the following steps:

1. Hold the line tight with your thumb, fingers, or the thumb button on your reel, depending on the type of rod and reel you are using.
2. Bring the rod back to the two O'clock position to "load" the rod. (Loading the rod means taking advantage of the energy in the rod material to help cast your bait or lure.)

Side-arm cast

3. Cast the rod toward your target and stop it with the rod tip pointing to the two o'clock position.

4. As you stop the rod, release your thumb, fingers, or the reel button so that the line shoots forward toward your target.

5. If you are using a bait-casting rod, be sure to put your thumb back on the line spool just as the line enters the water. Otherwise the spool will keep on spinning and you will end up with a tangled mess of line called a backlash.

For the side-arm cast, use the same motions and the same steps, but do it to the side instead of over your head.

Accurate casting will become a habit with practice. Excellent casters catch more fish, so practice, practice, practice.

Lawn Fishing

You can practice casting in your backyard or in an empty parking lot (just make sure there are no parked cars around; you wouldn't want a stray cast to damage them). A bait-casting or spinning rod will work best for this activity.

You will need to put some weight on the end of your line so that it will carry the line out when you cast. Don't use a hook in this exercise; you don't need it and it could be dangerous. You can use a small lead sinker or a rubber-coated weight made especially for this purpose. You'll find those sold in a bait and tackle shop.

Build yourself a target of some sort. Options are a sheet or towel on the ground, or perhaps a cardboard box or grocery bag. In a parking lot, you can draw a target on the pavement with chalk. Make the center of your target six inches in diameter. Draw some

more circles around it so you'll know how far off you are when you don't hit the center. (If it is a private lot, be sure to ask permission.)

Move back ten paces from your target and practice casting right to it. When you get so you can hit the target almost every time, back up five more paces and try again. Getting good? Then back up another five paces. Keep moving back as far as your rod, your strength, and your accuracy will allow.

Though fishing is not usually a competitive sport, you might want to make a game of lawn fishing. Devise a scoring system with points for hitting the target in the bull's-eye, fewer points for a near miss, and so forth. You can play this lawn-casting game with a friend. You'll both become better casters as you practice.

In the Water, But Where?

So, your hook is baited and you know how to cast, but now what? Toss it in the water, of course, and wait for the fish to bite. That's one choice, but by making some educated guesses as to where the fish might be, you'll have a lot better luck.

A wise old fisherman once said, "Fish are lazy and they don't like the sun." If you can remember this saying, it will help you figure out where the fish are likely to be in most any body of water.

"Fish Are Lazy"

Fish may not really be lazy, but they are cold-blooded creatures that eat lots of small meals so as to have enough strength to survive and grow. Therefore, they don't like to waste their valuable energy by swimming too far or too fast to get food (or to avoid being food for some other predator). This means that fish are usually found in spots where they can easily snatch food when it passes by, and where they can quickly hide if a lurking animal, bird, or larger fish is looking for dinner itself.

"They Don't Like the Sun"

Though fish probably don't have to worry about getting sunburned, they do have some good reasons for staying out of the sun. In water lit by strong sunlight, fish are more easily seen, which makes them more visible to birds, animals, and wily fishing persons. So, fish stay in the shadows whenever possible. Sometimes in a stream you'll see fish out in the sun feeding in the shallow water. Just remember, if you can see them, they can see you too, so you have to be sneaky to catch them.

Stream and River Hiding Places

Streams are dynamic places. Though the water always flows downhill, it doesn't all flow at the same speed. Even in a straight line across a stream, the water will be flowing at many different rates. The depth of the water, the shape of the stream bottom, and obstructions such as rocks and logs all affect the speed of the water. A fish will almost always place itself in a safe spot with good cover, where the flow of the water is slower and where food is likely to be drifting by. Thus, you'll find fish behind rocks where the stream flows around, at the heads of pools where food tumbles in, under overhanging banks where food floats by, and around logs and stumps.

If you wear polarized sunglasses, you'll be able to see the fish more easily under sunny or shady water.

A good angler (fisherman) is a careful observer of fish habitat (places they live). If the fishing is slow, or if you happen upon a fishing place without your tackle along, take some time to carefully notice your surroundings. Study places where fish might want to feed. Look for safe places for them to be and places where they can see and catch food easily without having to spend too much energy. Think about how the water is moving, where the deep holes might be, and what kind of cover is hanging over the bank. As you begin to look and really see these places, you´ll be surprised at how your "luck" will improve while fishing.

Pond and Lake Hiding Places

In a pond or lake there are many different places for fish to hide. Because the water is not flowing, fish don't have to worry so much about using excess energy, but they still have to be concerned about their safety. Also, as the sun warms the water, some fish will go into deeper water to stay in cooler temperatures. Depending on the type of fish, look for them next to a piling or under a dock or bridge, next to an undercut bank, in a weed or lily-pad bed, next to the mouth of a feeder stream or spring, or in cover such as sunken trees, rocks, or logs.

Always Be Thinking

Fishers who think and plan are more successful. Before you cast your bait or lure, try to imagine whether the place to where you are casting seems like a safe and easy place for a fish to get food. If the fish are there, and they are in the mood for a snack, you'll be much more likely to catch them.

WHAT MIGHT I CATCH ?

Rainbow Trout

Where They Live	What They Eat
In lakes and streams where the water is cool and clean. In streams they will usually be found near the faster water in the cover of rocks or logs. Because of state stocking programs, trout streams will often be marked by signs.	☆ worms ☆ grasshoppers/crickets ☆ salmon eggs ☆ artificial flies ☆ artificial spinners

Brown Trout

Where They Live	What They Eat
In lakes and streams where the water is cool and clean. They usually hide under a log or the stream bank. They are wary creatures that scare easily.	☆ grasshoppers/crickets ☆ artificial flies ☆ artificial spinners ☆ worms

Brook Trout

Where They Live	What They Eat
In lakes and streams where the water is cool and clean enough for them to survive. They need cooler water than rainbow and brown trout. These fish are usually small and fairly fragile. They can be found hiding behind rocks, stick, and logs. You'll have to sneak up on them.	☆ worms ☆ grasshoppers/crickets ☆ salmon eggs ☆ artificial flies ☆ artificial spinners

Lake Trout

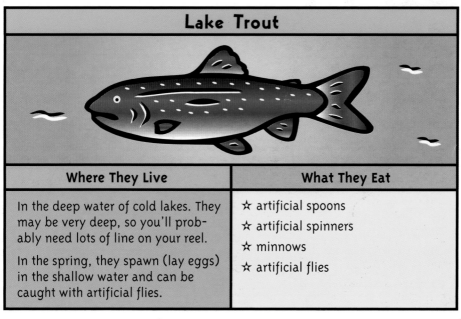

Where They Live	What They Eat
In the deep water of cold lakes. They may be very deep, so you'll probably need lots of line on your reel. In the spring, they spawn (lay eggs) in the shallow water and can be caught with artificial flies.	☆ artificial spoons ☆ artificial spinners ☆ minnows ☆ artificial flies

Largemouth Bass

Where They Live	What They Eat	
In lakes with warmer water. Usually found near the shore in weed beds, under lily pads, or around sunken logs, trees, and stumps. These fish are ferocious feeders, so when they take the bait they will give your rod quite a jolt.	☆ worms ☆ crayfish ☆ crickets ☆ surface plugs	☆ artificial worms ☆ popping bugs ☆ artificial flies

Smallmouth Bass

Where They Live	What They Eat	
In streams with water slightly cooler than preferred by their largemouth cousins. They like to be around rocks and boulders, and will chase your bait before they take it, so be patient.	☆ worms ☆ crayfish ☆ crickets ☆ minnows ☆ hellgrammites ☆ popping bugs	☆ underwater plugs ☆ artificial spinners ☆ artificial spoons

Catfish

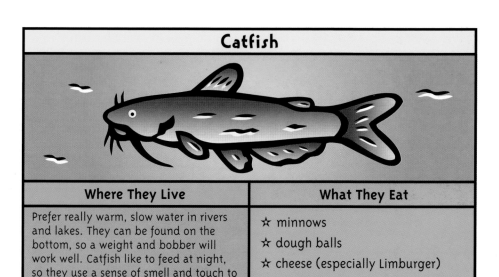

Where They Live	What They Eat
Prefer really warm, slow water in rivers and lakes. They can be found on the bottom, so a weight and bobber will work well. Catfish like to feed at night, so they use a sense of smell and touch to identify food. **Warning:** The dorsal and pectoral spines on a catfish carry a toxin that will irritate your hands. Use gloves when removing them from your hook.	☆ minnows ☆ dough balls ☆ cheese (especially Limburger) ☆ crayfish

Bluegill (bream)

Where They Live	What They Eat
Found along the shallow edges of lakes and ponds, in weeds and lily pads.	Being the smallest "kids" on the block, they have to be willing to eat most anything. This means they take most any bait. ☆ worms ☆ corn ☆ crickets/grasshoppers ☆ marshmallows ☆ hot dog ☆ popping bugs ☆ cheese ☆ small spinners ☆ dough balls ☆ artificial flies

Perch

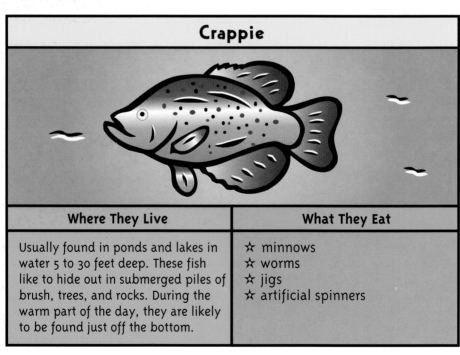

Where They Live	What They Eat
In lakes and ponds with slightly deeper water; larger perch like depths of 10 to 50 feet. These fish hang out together in schools, so where there is one, there are probably more.	☆ minnows ☆ crayfish ☆ worms ☆ artificial spinners ☆ grasshoppers ☆ jigs

Crappie

Where They Live	What They Eat
Usually found in ponds and lakes in water 5 to 30 feet deep. These fish like to hide out in submerged piles of brush, trees, and rocks. During the warm part of the day, they are likely to be found just off the bottom.	☆ minnows ☆ worms ☆ jigs ☆ artificial spinners

Sunfish

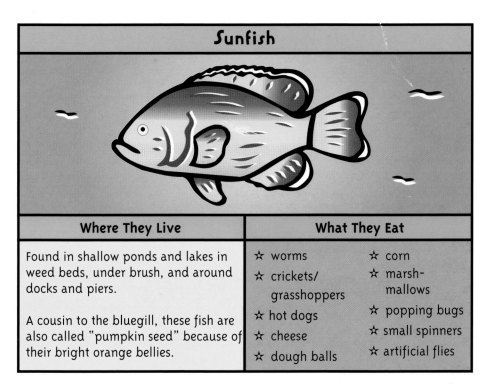

Where They Live	What They Eat	
Found in shallow ponds and lakes in weed beds, under brush, and around docks and piers. A cousin to the bluegill, these fish are also called "pumpkin seed" because of their bright orange bellies.	☆ worms ☆ crickets/ grasshoppers ☆ hot dogs ☆ cheese ☆ dough balls	☆ corn ☆ marsh- mallows ☆ popping bugs ☆ small spinners ☆ artificial flies

Walleye

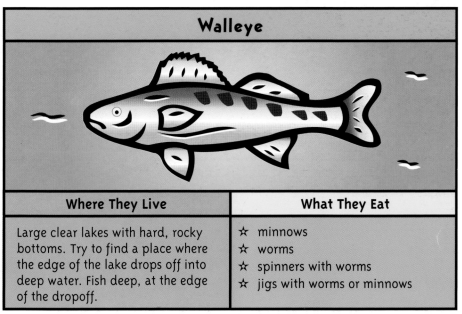

Where They Live	What They Eat
Large clear lakes with hard, rocky bottoms. Try to find a place where the edge of the lake drops off into deep water. Fish deep, at the edge of the dropoff.	☆ minnows ☆ worms ☆ spinners with worms ☆ jigs with worms or minnows

Muskellunge

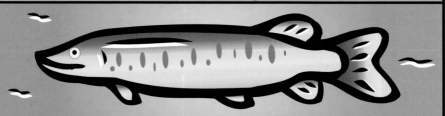

Where They Live	What They Eat
Spend most of their time in the deep water of lakes, but they like to feed in the weeds and shallow shoals. Most muskies are caught while trolling (slowly pulling your lure along) behind a moving boat, but they can be taken by a bait-casting or heavy spinning rod. If you catch a muskie, be very careful removing it from your hook. Its teeth are very sharp and can cut your hands.	☆ minnows ☆ worms ☆ spinners with worms ☆ jigs with worms or minnows

Northern Pike

Where They Live	What They Eat
Can be found in slow-moving streams and the weedy shallows of lakes—under logs and lily pads and beside stumps. They are aggressive feeders that eat other forms of aquatic life. They even eat small ducks and muskrats! If you catch a pike, be very careful removing it from your hook. Its teeth are very sharp and can cut your hands.	☆ minnows ☆ frogs (real or artificial) ☆ large artificial plugs (under-water and surface) ☆ big spoons

WHAT DO I DO WITH THE FISH?

YOU'VE LEARNED YOUR fishing lessons well, and now you've caught a fish, or maybe a few fish. So now what? You can keep the fish or let it go. Or you can keep it for just a minute or so and then release it. Let's examine some possibilities.

Release It

Unless you plan to cook and eat what you catch (or give your catch to someone else who will), you'll probably want to release the fish so it can be caught again another day. Some lakes and streams are set apart as "catch and release" or "fish for fun" only. In these special-regulation areas, you'll be expected to release everything you catch.

If you want to release a fish in a way that it can live to grow and be caught again, you'll need to be careful how you handle it. As you remove the hook, hold the fish just behind its head, not around its belly. And be careful not to squeeze the fish too hard. You don't want to damage its vital organs. Try to hold the fish in the water while you remove the hook, but if you have to take it out of the water, don't keep it out any longer than absolutely necessary. Remember, the fish can't breathe in the air, just like you can't breathe under the water.

If you have hooked the fish in the lip, remove the hook gently with your fingers or with a pair of needle-nose pliers. Be sure not to hook yourself in the process!

If your fish has swallowed the hook, use a hook disgorger or a small stick to carefully work the hook out. If you can't easily remove it, just cut off the line at the fish's mouth. The hook will dissolve in just a few days. You'll lose a hook but you may save a fish.

Hold the fish underwater with its head pointed upstream (the direction from which the water is flowing). This will allow water to flow into its mouth and through the gills. The oxygen will give it energy to revive. Allow the fish to swim away under its own power when it is ready. If it turns on its side or upside down, it is not yet revived. Point the fish upstream and hold it there until it is strong enough to swim away.

Properly releasing a fish is a good fish conservation habit. Practice learning to do it correctly and teach your friends.

Photograph It

If you are fishing with a friend and you have your camera along, you might want to take a picture of your fish before you release it. Remember, the sun should be behind the person taking the picture so you and your fish will be well lighted for the photograph. Also, try to do this fairly quickly as the fish can't breathe while you are snapping away.

Draw It

Many old fishing lodges are filled with "fish boards." Instead of keeping and stuffing their fish, many anglers choose to find an old board and draw a picture of their fish to hang as a trophy. If you plan to do this, take a quick moment to measure your fish and take a photo of it. This information will help you as you draw your "trophy" later.

Eat It

Storing Your Fish

If you decide you want to have a fish dinner (or breakfast or lunch), the first step after catching your fish is keeping it fresh until you have time to clean and cook it. Some people use a fish stringer, which is a thin rope or a chain with clips that look like large safety pins. The rope or clips go through the mouth and gills, and the fish are kept in the water until the end of the fishing day.

A better way to keep your fish is to kill them quickly by thumping them on the head with a stick or rock and then storing them in a cooler with ice. Do not cook or eat fish that have not been properly stored. It could make you sick.

Cleaning Your Fish

Before cooking your fish it will need to be cleaned. This involves taking out the internal organs, called "gutting" the fish, and removing the scales, called "scaling" the fish. Get an adult helper who has cleaned fish before to show you how to do these two things. The sooner you clean the fish after you kill it, the fresher it will taste when you cook it.

Fish can be cooked whole (with bones) or filleted [pronounced fil-LAYED] (without bones). Smaller fish usually need to be cooked whole, but larger fish can be filleted so you don't have to worry about the bones when you are eating. Get an adult helper to show you how to do this, as well.

Cooking Your Fish

Frying It

Roll the fish in corn meal or pancake flour with a little salt and pepper. Heat some cooking oil in a skillet large enough to hold the fish. When the oil is good and hot (just before it smokes), carefully place your fish into the oil and fry it until it is golden brown. It is done when the meat flakes off easily with a fork. Take the fish out, place it on a paper towel to drain the oil, then dig in and eat while it is hot. If you haven't filleted your fish, be careful not to swallow any bones.

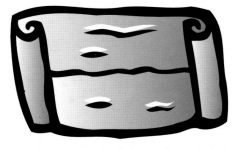

Baking It in a Campfire

Put some salt and pepper on the inside of your fish and roll it up in several layers of aluminum foil. If you happen to have some celery, onion, or green pepper, chop them up and stuff them inside the fish or lay them on top. Roll up the ends of the foil to make a tight cooking container.

Let your campfire burn until you have a good bed of coals. Place the fish down in the coals and cover them up. How fast your fish cooks depends on its weight, whether it is whole or filleted, and how hot the coals are. As a guideline, allow about 10-15 minutes of cooking time per pound. Carefully open the foil packet and test for flakiness with a fork. When your fish is done, roll back the foil and enjoy your campfire dinner. There are hundreds of different ways to prepare fish for eating. Check your kitchen recipe books to discover some new and interesting ways to cook them. Buy fish at the store and practice at home.

Making a fishing log book is a project you can do indoors on a rainy day or a winter day when you can't get out to your favorite fishing hole. Keeping good records about the places you fish is fun, and it might prove to be useful on future fishing expeditions. "Gee, I wonder what the fish were biting at Trophy Fish Pond in April of last year?" If you've kept a good log, you won't have to remember. Just look it up!

Find a three-ring binder or some other kind of notebook that you can clip pages into. Then design some log sheets and find a way to have multiple copies made. This is a project you might be able to do on your home computer.

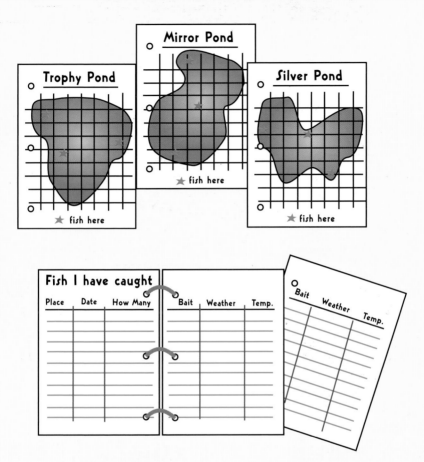

Make a separate page for each pond, lake, or stream you fish in. Make some extra copies for new places you will explore in the future. On one side of the paper, record your fishing data for each trip to that particular spot. You might want to keep a record of things like date fished, time of day you caught fish, number of fish caught, size of fish, kind of fish, hook size used, bait or lure used, weather conditions, and temperature. On the back of each page you might create some grids (like graph paper) to use for drawing small maps of the specific places on streams and lakes where you found your fish.

Other Activity Books from

Gibbs Smith Junior

COOKING ON A STICK
Campfire Recipes for Kids
by Linda White
illustrated by Fran Lee
48 pages, $8.95

SLEEPING IN A SACK
Camping Activities for Kids
by Linda White
illustrated by Fran Lee
64 pages, $10.00

HIDING IN A FORT
Backyard Retreats for Kids
by Lawson Drinkard
illustrated by Fran Lee
48 pages, $8.95

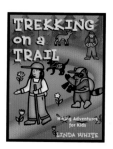

TREKKING ON A TRAIL
Hiking Adventures for Kids
by Linda White
illustrated by Fran Lee
64 pages, $9.95

Available at bookstores or directly from the publisher.
GIBBS SMITH, PUBLISHER
1.800.748.5439/www.gibbs-smith.com